Poems From Buckinghamshire

Edited By Jess Giaffreda

First published in Great Britain in 2019 by:

 Young**Writers**®
Est. 1991

Young Writers
Remus House
Coltsfoot Drive
Peterborough
PE2 9BF
Telephone: 01733 890066
Website: www.youngwriters.co.uk

FOREWORD

Here at Young Writers, we love to let imaginations run wild and creativity go crazy. Our aim is to encourage young people to get their creative juices flowing and put pen to paper. Each competition is tailored to the relevant age group, hopefully giving each pupil the inspiration and incentive to create their own piece of creative writing, whether it's a poem or a short story. By allowing them to see their own work in print, we know their confidence and love for the written word will grow.

For our latest competition Poetry Wonderland, we invited primary school pupils to create wild and wonderful poems on any topic they liked – the only limits were the limits of their imagination! Using poetry as their magic wand, these young poets have conjured up worlds, creatures and situations that will amaze and astound or scare and startle! Using a variety of poetic forms of their own choosing, they have allowed us to get a glimpse into their vivid imaginations. We hope you enjoy wandering through the wonders of this book as much as we have.

★ CONTENTS ★

Brooklands Farm Primary School, Milton Keynes

Luca Williams (8)	1
Iggy Ellams-Marshall (10)	2
Elizabeth Hannah Thelwell (10)	4
Niya Nair (10)	6
Zain Khodair (10)	8
Arnav Prashant Gavankar (10)	10
Aleksandra Jurewicz (9)	12
Shahyan Abbas Ghasemi (11)	14
Imogen Pearl McMillan (8)	16
Ayomide Dada (9)	18
Reeka Chanelle Manglicmot (9)	20
Janelle Allison (11)	22
Martha Morrison (10)	24
Philippe-Gael Gisa Kabera (10)	26
Kaitlyn Yan En Teh (9)	28
Isaac McCulloch (11)	30
Caraleena Williams (10)	32
Oliver Nichols (8)	34
Ethan Patey (9)	36
Rania Raashid (9)	38
Lexi Spensley (10)	39
Noah Ben-Bassat (8)	40
Mia Woodards (8)	42
Alex Penosh (8)	43
Amelia Williams (8)	44
Ewan MacKay (8)	45
Eleanor Grace Collins (9)	46
Sadie Ellis (9)	47
Elsie Lindley (9)	48
Hannah Goodwin (8)	49
Logan Sewett (8)	50
Lucas Morris (9)	52
Amelia Jefferson (9)	53

Chahat Gurbani (8)	54
Austeja Poznanskaite (9)	55
Grace (9)	56
Lily-Grace Pink (9)	57
Reyansh Totala (8)	58
Tilly Locke (9)	59
Nduka Jason C Okomba (9)	60
Danielle Donovan (8)	61
Asia Nandoo (9)	62
Izzie Harvey (8)	64
Kendra Evans (9)	65
Zofia Natalia Pulido (9)	66
Ellie Hyde (9)	67
Rory Sims (9)	68
Dakota-Blue Young (10)	69
Faith Ashington (8)	70
Aimee Nunn (9)	71
Tristan Law (9)	72
Amielia Caroline Kay (10)	73
Ezra Sana Hashemi (9)	74
Jaime Cross (9)	75
Selin Kocum (9)	76
Erin Ebrahim (9)	77
Ruby Chambers (9)	78
Aleena Farooqui (10)	79
Hamsini Bacchu (8)	80
Dalitso Mpepo (10)	81
Muhammad Hassan Maher (8)	82
Sandra Sreekumar (9)	83
Asher Peter Buluku Roberts (10)	84
Megan Brooke Denehan (9)	85
Rachel Grunwell (9)	86
Mason Woolf (9)	87
Jenai Allison (8)	88
Daisy Lowen (9)	89

Kayhan Moradi (8)	90
Jack Morris (8)	91
Michael Sagar (8)	92
Dhioni Tailor (9)	93
Leon Moradi (9)	94
Skye Jessica Astle (7)	95
Ameya Polavajram (7)	96
Annabella Okafor (7)	97
Jake Coxhill (9)	98
Erin Spensley (7)	99
Anaya Umer (7)	100
Isabella Purdy-Cross (9)	101
Hrithvik Daggu (9)	102
Shannon Lavery-Singh (7)	103
Isla Lloyd (7)	104
Hattie Hughes- Stone (7)	105
Emilia Kendall (8)	106
Olivia Zajkowska (7)	107
Mathys Levet (9)	108
Niamh Carrington (7)	109
Amelie (7)	110
Alfie James Gordon (7)	111
Callan Lindsay (7)	112
Eve Gallagher (7)	113
Theo M Salifu (9)	114
Grace French (7)	115
Alfie Sanderson (7)	116
Isabella Derham (7)	117
Taylor Dunn (9)	118
Bella Pringle (7)	119
Kai Buckley (7)	120

Giffard Park Primary School, Giffard Park

Jamie Saunders (10)	121
Samuel Inwood (10)	122
Talitha Grace Mkwashi (10)	124
Grace Ellery (11)	126
Rebecca Gill (11)	128
Francesca Jane Sicorello (11)	130
Grace Black (10)	132
Elain Krayem (11)	133
Ella Glass (10)	134

Emily Gunn (10)	135
Kacper Oskar Zak (10)	136
Jamie Windebank (10)	137
Chloe Brown (10)	138
Sahl Fowzulameen (10)	139
Jasmine Charlotte Wareing (10)	140
Dragos Mihai Pascu (10)	141
Jessica Asumbwe (10)	142
Alicia Faid (11)	143
Finley Wirth (10)	144
Grace Lillie Mundye (11)	145
Ella Angell (10)	146
Rory McCauley (10)	147
Jack Harry Lawson (10)	148
Amber Hussain (10)	149
Tabitha Hancock (10)	150
Toby Jarvis (10)	151
Alfie James Ray (10)	152
Jack Mitchell (10)	153
Alfie King (11)	154
Katie Hawes (11)	155
Shammah Doka (11)	156
Nadina Satala (10)	157
Jacquiline Badu (10)	158

Hughenden Primary School, Hughenden Valley

Anna L	159

Ivingswood Academy, Greenway

Emily Read (10)	160
Tayla Stanley (10)	161
Bilal Jarcheh (10)	162
Abdullah Hussain (10)	163
Lincoln Savage (11)	164
Zainab Zeeshan Butt (10)	165
Ayman Butt (10)	166
Isha Mirza (10)	167
Izaac McConnell (10)	168
Mason Dickinson (11)	169
Zaina Riasat (10)	170
Logan Jordan (10)	171

Long Meadow School, Milton Keynes

Nicole Hargreaves (10)	172
Joshua George (9)	173
Anushree Pathak (10)	174
Dhanvi Joy Choksi (10)	176
Nana Nuru (9)	177
Anna Batchelor (10)	178
Jaysha Malika Coulthurst-Wood (9)	179
Evie Durn (9)	180
Max Medley (10)	181
Lily May Walsh (9)	182
Imogene Rainbow Salamon (10)	183
Mohith Ram Sigirisetti (10)	184
Mia Farebrother (10)	185
Logan George Freeman (9)	186
Dylan Jake Jemmett (9)	187
Oheneba Kofi-Baah Dompreh (9)	188
Alfie James Ratcliffe (9)	189
William Robertson (9)	190

★ The Poems ★

If I Were In Charge Of The World

If I were in charge of the world,
I'd cancel bullying every week,
School and also strict teachers!

If I were in charge of the world,
There'd be free, never-ending V-Bucks
And I'd meet really famous YouTubers in real life

If I were in charge of the world,
You wouldn't have zoos,
You wouldn't have detention,
You wouldn't have guns
Or homework
You wouldn't even have jobs

If I were in charge of the world,
Sweets and chocolate would be vegetables
All people would live in big houses
And people who sometimes forgot to wash,
And sometimes forgot to dance
Would still be allowed to be in charge of the world.

Luca Williams (8)

Brooklands Farm Primary School, Milton Keynes

1

Birth Of A Hero

I started school when I was four,
With Raaid and Rishet, I became fast friends
I learnt ABCs, counting and more
I thought, *I hope school never ends!*

In Year 1, there was much more work,
Learning column addition was what I achieved,
Less time to jump around and be a berk,
New Brooklands values - open, grow, believe

Now, Year 2 was much more tricky,
Growing my maths by learning division
I went to the chocolate factory and got all sticky
Plus, I learnt how to write with far more precision

My time in Year 3 came with higher expectations,
I made sure I looked out for the younger years
I studied the rainforests in far away nations,
And read about Spartans with big pointy spears

In Year 4, I studied more times and divide,
And read how the Romans were an unstoppable
force

My mummy married Pete and was a beautiful bride
It made me so excited, I cried, of course

With Year 5 came new glasses that helped me to see,
I got all my times tables saved in my head
Being on the school council filled me with glee
All of this work made me ready for bed

I think Year 6 will be a bit more hard,
Learning things like BODMAS has left me vexed
I'll grow my writing until I'm as good as the bard,
I'm ready to face whatever comes next.

Iggy Ellams-Marshall (10)
Brooklands Farm Primary School, Milton Keynes

School

I started school when I was three,
I was playful and creative,
I loved to sing and was eager
To learn
Along with being imaginative

In Year 1, I made new friends,
Still playful and creative
I was full of life,
And I was learning new phrases
I was small and talkative,
Determined to show that I could achieve

When Year 2 came running around the corner,
I had grown a little more
My confidence lacked
But my friends were always there
To push me through that door

In Year 3, I was calmer than before,
Wanting to weave more of my learning journey
I started to grow,

And started to know more than before
My confidence had been boosted high

In Year 5, I was tall
But my friends still towered over me
I learnt about Harry Potter
Which at the time was my dream
Titanic Day was amazing,
With Mrs Peasnall running down the corridor

Year 6 is yet to come soon,
Bye-bye Brooklands,
Hello Oakgrove School
Brooklands will remain in my heart,
For as long as my short-term memory will let me
I have grown so much now,
But there is still more time for improvement.

Elizabeth Hannah Thelwell (10)

Brooklands Farm Primary School, Milton Keynes

The Change

Y1 was the start
I made some friends
A big part of life
I still had bends
In Year 1 I was still small
Trying to be the best of all

Y2 was good at school
I turned very calm
Some of the subjects were very cool
As I looked at the growing of my palm
I did a lot of hard work
Even though there were tears

Y3 was the next stage
I had to balance writing on a page
I worked hard to be in a good mood
And tried not to be rude
I had to continue with my writing journey
Even with obstacles

Y4 was my favourite part
My subject was fancy art

I tried really hard to achieve
But my learning journey I could not leave
I introduced myself to many things
Even things with unhappy endings

In Y5 there was no fuss
As I was saying hello to the 11+
In Y5 I was tall
Trying to tower over them all
Individual was my word
And I stuck to it like a cord

I found Y6 was like building bricks
Also applying many tricks
Being strong and powerful
And individual
I had a lot of fun
But my work is not yet done.

Niya Nair (10)
Brooklands Farm Primary School, Milton Keynes

Growing In My School

In Year 1, I was full of questions;
but I was also giving lots of suggestions.
An exciting thing to have were those adventures,
by the end, I had tons of treasures.

In Year 2, I had a blast;
irritatingly, it went so fast!
We went on some amazing trips,
after handing in all of those slips.

In Year 3, we went swimming every Tuesday;
I must say, they had a nicely decorated walkway.
My favourite project was on natural disasters,
hence we saw lots of forecasters.

Year 4 was definitely not a bore,
I would love to have stayed there for more!
We learnt lots about the Romans,
and for Golden Tea, I would often get chosen.

When we were studying maths in Year 5,
I found out the answer was forty-five.
My favourite time was at Harry Potter World,

he did his magic when he picked up his wand and swirled.

Just one more year until secondary school,
I will use primary like a stepping stool.

Zain Khodair (10)
Brooklands Farm Primary School, Milton Keynes

The Change

The day I began school
At the age of six
I was little and immature
But still determined
Working hard, I learnt in Year 1
Showing that I could grow my work

In Year 2,
Still so small,
But I did it all
We went to the chocolate factory
And had a great time
My teachers told me to be calm,
But I couldn't hold it in at all

As we came up in Year 3,
Getting ready for Key Stage 2
It was hard to be balanced
And know what to do
As I was only a little bit tall

In Year 4, I had to achieve
As it was my belief

Miss Cooper helped me a lot,
So this was the best of all
I was medium-sized so I got the prize

When I was in Year 5
I was individual
A lot of responsibility as I was so tall
This was my most independent year
As this was my hardest year

Now it is my last year here,
I have learnt so much
And now I have to be strong and powerful.

Arnav Prashant Gavankar (10)
Brooklands Farm Primary School, Milton Keynes

The Change In School!

I came when I was five,
And felt very small
But even then, I wanted to arrive,
At a school where I could be myself

When I was six,
I wanted to learn
So my teacher Miss Murphy taught me some tricks,
Like 3x10=30

This was a change,
I had to change schools
It felt so strange,
But I still managed to grow

My word in Year 4,
Was 'achieve'
I achieved new friendships and the ability to roar,
And also grew smarter and taller as well

My class teacher was Miss Hearn,
All throughout Year 5, I have grown also with my
size

With Miss Hearn, it was easy to learn,
As I prepared for my 11+ and SATs this year

My final year is Year 6,
Where I've done my 11+ and learning for SATs
My teacher, Miss Sheridan, will secure me like a
load of bricks
I will try my best to impress her and be strong and
powerful.

Aleksandra Jurewicz (9)

Brooklands Farm Primary School, Milton Keynes

Six Years Of Change

Year 1 when I was very small,
Hoping once to be above them all
At first, I was very shy,
Not wanting to say a single lie

Year 2 at Brooklands Farm,
Was where I made my friends
Who taught me how to be calm,
Till the very end

Year 3 was my first year in KS2,
And I didn't know what to do
I learned advance in maths and writing,
And balanced them both to my liking

My favourite year by far was Year 4,
And it definitely was not a bore
Ancient Egypt and endangered animals
Released my skill in writing and art

The hardest year was Year 5,
As this was the year I had to thrive
And there was no time for any fuss,

As I was doing the 11+

Now I am in Year 6,
And learned life is like building bricks
And that life can't only be easy
So we should stop being grouchy.

Shahyan Abbas Ghasemi (11)
Brooklands Farm Primary School, Milton Keynes

If I Were In Charge Of The World

If I were in charge of the world,
I'd cancel the seven times table,
Blunt pencils,
Cuts and bruises,
Dry glue sticks
And also losing the page of the book you're
reading

If I were in charge of the world,
Penguins would live in England,
Fire wouldn't be able to burn down houses,
It wouldn't matter if you spell a word wrong in a
spelling test,
Books would appear out of thin air
And pencils would change colour while you write

If I were in charge of the world,
We wouldn't have choking,
Someone accidentally stepping on your fingers,
Tests,

Wrong answers
Or shoelaces

If I were in charge of the world,
Chocolate cake,
Ice cream
And sticky toffee pudding would be healthy
And not doing homework
And going on an aeroplane without a ticket would
be good.

Imogen Pearl McMillan (8)
Brooklands Farm Primary School, Milton Keynes

Change

So much has changed,
I have gone through so much
From being bullied and shouted at
But school has been amazing so far

I started at a small height,
But still very bright
I was only five with not many friends
But I was used to it

Year 2 was something else,
I had my seventh birthday party, which was
amazing
I was pushing myself to the limit,
But I had to be calm

Then Year 3 was just around the corner,
It was scary,
Coming up those stairs,
I had to be brave,
And positive

Year 4 just knocked at my door,
Learning about ancient Egypt
And why people were slaves

Year 5 was baffling,
I had to develop new relationships
With new teachers,
But I had worked it out

Now I am in Year 6,
My last year
But I will always have Brooklands in my heart!

Ayomide Dada (9)
Brooklands Farm Primary School, Milton Keynes

Be The Person To Change Children's Lives

All around us are an abundance of different faces,
Everything is never the same, they're unique.
Everywhere we go, all known places,
There are things that are different, some you can seek.

Listen to my prayers please,
Let's not have a raging dispute.
For equality, my heart it grieves,
It's possible, my brain knows it's absolute.

All around us everywhere,
Are people finding a resolution.
For homeless children thinking it's not fair,
So we all have to make the right decision.

This must be your priority,
Because homeless children have nothing to do.
Life is not a minority,
If we all help children break through.

From utter sadness and misery they flee,
So what can you do as an individual?
They're lonely, victims of depravity,
Every little change is visible.

Reeka Chanelle Manglicmot (9)

Brooklands Farm Primary School, Milton Keynes

School Changes

I came to Brooklands when I was five,
And didn't understand much
I thought the teachers would deprive
The imagination I had clutched

In Year 2, I grew taller,
And became smarter
At times I would make jokes and holler,
But I still had a kind heart

During Year 3, I tried working even harder,
To achieve my goals
But sometimes I wondered,
What would be my future role?

When I was in Year 4,
I never gave up
Learning new things was never a bore,
If I looked at education close up

Throughout Year 5,
I got to know Miss Hearn

Who made my ideas come alive,
And made my troubles burn

Lastly, in Year 6,
I learnt that sometimes I could be wrong
And that life was like building bricks
So when I say, "I can't", I will remember to be
strong.

Janelle Allison (11)
Brooklands Farm Primary School, Milton Keynes

My Learning Journey

I started school when I was four,
I was playful and creative
I loved to sing, I loved to play
And was imaginative

In Year 1, I left my friends and went
To a new school and met new people
Though I was a little small, I was taller than my
friends
And that was pretty cool

In Year 2, I learnt some more
And became intent to learn
We went to cool places like Cadbury World,
And met some cute owls

In Year 3, we learnt about Greeks and the
Victorians
We went to the botanical gardens
And held some reptiles

In Year 4, I learnt about Egyptians
And how they worshipped their gods

Then it was endangered animals,
And some of them were frogs

In Year 5, we entered Harry Potter's wizarding
world
Then the Titanic sinking,
And Year 6 is yet to come!

Martha Morrison (10)
Brooklands Farm Primary School, Milton Keynes

The Individual I Want To Be

I'm going to be the change I want to be,
Make a better school for you and me
I won't be kept locked up, but fly free,
A bright future I can see

Listen to my questions please,
For who knows what I can achieve?
I only want to be happy, not to grieve
I know it's impossible but I still believe

No one will always agree,
Everyone has different opinions, like you and me
Or cross the biggest seam
Beyond the islands, individuals I can see

Please show no animosities,
To any person or minorities
As different as a star and Mercury,
An individual group of trees

From the conflicted and the underseen,
And the things we don't mean
Be clean and seen
An end to relying on people,
An individual, that is my plea.

Philippe-Gael Gisa Kabera (10)
Brooklands Farm Primary School, Milton Keynes

Be The Individual You Want To See

Be the individual you want to be,
A caring heart and a helpful hand
Makes a better school for you and me
Listen to my words, I might be right, I might not be
But make a better school for you and me

I might be right or wrong, but I still believe that
you and me can
Make a school a better place for you and me
Where children can roam free
But listen to my words please,
Who knows what this verse can achieve?
For a caring heart and a helpful hand,
You can make a better place for you and me

Don't be mean, don't bully, for we can change your
life fully
An individual I can be, an individual you can be
With a friend and a teacher,
You and me can make a change

We shouldn't have wars or fights,
I want peace for you and me.

Kaitlyn Yan En Teh (9)

Brooklands Farm Primary School, Milton Keynes

Grow

I started school at the age of four,
I needed to make friends
I thought it would be hard,
But it was easy
With the help of my teachers
I was playful with my new friends,
Especially on the climbing frame

As I moved up to Year 1,
I started to get louder and more energetic,
I had a bigger playground
So I had more freedom to run around
With no gates surrounding me
As I was Year 1,
I got to join the school in the hall

As I went to Year 2,
I got scared but I got used to it
When I was in Year 2,
I started to grow a bit,
And had more trust with my teachers

In Year 2,
I started to learn how to work harder and harder

Moving up to Year 3,
I wasn't so keen,
But it was for me.

Isaac McCulloch (11)

Brooklands Farm Primary School, Milton Keynes

Change

When I was four,
I went to school
I learnt a lot throughout the school
I grew and grew
Until I was filled with joy
Although I was shy,
I stood up for all my friends

Now I have to say goodbye,
'Cause now I'm moving to another school
I was still shy in Year 1 and 2,
But getting bigger and stronger in Year 3
In the past, learning about all new things,
Greek mythology,
The rainforest and the Great Fire of London was
pretty cool

Moving up to Year 4,
Listening to each other and learning some more
Making more friends was lots of fun
Titanic and Egypt, lots to do

In Year 6, still having an amazing time,
Learning about the brain and World War II,
The journey still carries on.

Caraleena Williams (10)

Brooklands Farm Primary School, Milton Keynes

If I Could Change The World

If I could change the world,
I'd cancel people dying
Guns, bad dreams and nightmares

If I could change the world,
There'd be unlimited healthy food for everyone,
Amazing schools and holidays wherever we
wanted

If I could change the world,
You wouldn't have reading books,
You wouldn't have homeless people,
You wouldn't have the smell of fish,
Sharks would be vegetarian,
And hug people when they surfed instead of biting
them

If I could change the world,
Chocolate ice cream would become a fruit
And Coke would be water
And Fanta would become orange juice

And a person who is sometimes late,
And even forgot to wash
Would still be allowed to change the world.

Oliver Nichols (8)

Brooklands Farm Primary School, Milton Keynes

Change

The change that is in my mind,
To tackle it, everyone needs to be combined
The new class, it's fine with me
Be the individual you want to be

I'm getting hungry, when's lunch?
We are role models, the whole bunch
I love my new friends,
I have still remembered how to count in tens!

Open, grow, believe,
That's how I achieve
Only sometimes, I grieve,
But I will never leave

Oh, the harder learning,
There really should be some earning
Not that I even care,
I don't want a dare

With my mum saying, "Do this! Do that!"
I just want to give a dog a pat

I love my life and me,
I love all of 5B!

Ethan Patey (9)

Brooklands Farm Primary School, Milton Keynes

If I Were In Charge Of The World

If I were in charge of the world,
I would get rid of detentions, homework, the
behaviour chart
And definitely maths!
If I were in charge of the world,
Life would be so much easier with free Chrome
books and iPads,
Not waking up so early and getting free money,
So I could go to Dubai,
And get free chocolate and sweets
And sticky doughnuts!
If I were in charge of the world,
I would get rid of Fortnite, people that nag me,
And always no school on Monday mornings
If I were in charge of the world,
I would try not to go on the internet for very long,
Try not to ignore people,
I would try not to eat much chocolate or sweets
And try to make sure my family has a voice.

Rania Raashid (9)
Brooklands Farm Primary School, Milton Keynes

Be The Person In Your Dream

Be the person in your dream,
There's only one ingredient to the recipe
Being an individual is what to be,
Why though? We shall see

Being an individual is being strong,
However, there is no right or wrong
Being an individual doesn't take long,
Just listen to these words, it's not a song

You may not agree,
Some work alone, others in a team
You will climb up the highest learning journey,
Beyond explorer, voyager you'll be

Being an individual isn't all to retrieve,
You'll need to open, grow and believe
You heard me right, that's how you achieve,
So go weave your learning journey, weave, weave,
weave.

Lexi Spensley (10)
Brooklands Farm Primary School, Milton Keynes

If I Were In Charge Of The World

If I were in charge of the world,
I would want no unicorns and no gymnastics
As well as cancer, no Fortnite, smoking,
No short school lessons

I would cancel nightmares
I would cancel guns, people dying,
Get rid of murderers

Unlimited food, unlimited drinks
I would cancel football
I would love to have a happy family,
No rudeness, no swearing, no sadness

I would cancel rainy days,
No homeless people, no healthy food
Just midnight feasts

I would give homeless people billions of money
And a place to live
And a vacation to rest

And have time to relax
And have a drink
And also watch a show.

Noah Ben-Bassat (8)
Brooklands Farm Primary School, Milton Keynes

If I Were In Charge Of The World

If I were in charge of the world,
I'd cancel school uniforms for girls
Allergy shots and make sure only police have guns
And no boring subjects in school

If I were in charge of the world,
Everything in the shops would be free,
There would be areas where boys couldn't go
No teachers and no brothers
Boys would have to go to boring school,
Unlike girls who would go to fun school
And get to leave when they wanted to

If I were in charge of the world,
Chocolate would be your five a day
Strawberry laces would be vegetables
Fortnite would be part of learning only for girls
Only boys would have to wear uniforms.

Mia Woodards (8)
Brooklands Farm Primary School, Milton Keynes

If I Could Rule The World

If I were the ruler of the world,
I'd cancel golf, unicorns,
Warning two and also the school,
If I were the ruler of the world,
There'd be no black holes,
No rules and no dancing.
If I were the ruler of the world,
You wouldn't have cancer,
You wouldn't have to shrink,
You wouldn't have masks or dancing
You wouldn't even have singing.
If I were the ruler of the world,
A chocolate cream sundae would be a vegetable,
All guns would be gone,
And a person who sometimes forgot to brush,
And sometimes forgot to flush,
Would still be allowed to be in charge of the world.

Alex Penosh (8)
Brooklands Farm Primary School, Milton Keynes

If I Ruled The World

If I ruled the world,
I'd cancel illness, smoking, bacteria and also rabies

If I ruled the world,
There'd be games at school, longer days and
happy families

If I ruled the world,
You wouldn't have poor people,
You wouldn't have knives,
You wouldn't have swearing,
Or guns, you wouldn't even have war

If I ruled the world,
A chocolate bar would be a vegetable,
All of the different kinds of ice cream would be
healthy,
And a person who sometimes forgot to brush their
teeth,
And sometimes forgot to flush,
Would still be allowed to be in charge of the world.

Amelia Williams (8)
Brooklands Farm Primary School, Milton Keynes

If I Ruled The World

If I were in charge of the world,
I'd cancel Fortnite, drums,
Fireworks and books

If I were in charge of the world,
There'd be no guns, knives and writing

If I were in charge of the world,
You wouldn't have bedtime
You wouldn't have lunch
You wouldn't have fruit or jobs
You would have ice cream mixed with lollipops

If I were in charge of the world,
A sticky toffee pudding would be a vegetable
All sisters are taught at home
And people who sometimes forget to drink,
And sometimes forget to flush
Would still be allowed to be in charge of the world.

Ewan MacKay (8)

Brooklands Farm Primary School, Milton Keynes

If I Could Rule The World

If I could rule the world,
I'd cancel littering, cigarettes,
Swear words and also illness

If I could rule the world,
There'd be bigger days, holidays more often
And everyone would be nice and crazy

If I could rule the world,
You wouldn't have school uniforms
You wouldn't have Coke
You wouldn't have Diet Coke
Or homeless people
You wouldn't even have rudeness

If I could rule the world,
A sweet would be a vegetable
And a person who sometimes forgot to flush,
And sometimes forgot to share
Would still be allowed to rule the world.

Eleanor Grace Collins (9)
Brooklands Farm Primary School, Milton Keynes

Change Is Fun!

Be strong, independent and always have faith
You change all the time,
Being an individual is a lot of hard work

Listen to your heart,
Let your colours shine
You could be the finest individual in the year
Change isn't scary,
Change is your time to shine

Sometimes we have to accept change,
If we want to move forward
We think we can only change clothes, well we're
wrong
Your heart and feelings can change too

Individuality isn't hard,
Just listen to these words
That will help you across your journey
Strong, powerful, sense of self and resilience.

Sadie Ellis (9)
Brooklands Farm Primary School, Milton Keynes

Individuals

Be the change I want to see,
A better individual I can be
A place my mistakes can roam free,
Make individuals better than they used to be

Listen to my advice please,
Who knows what this verse achieves?
For individuals, my heart agrees,
It's possible, my heart believes

Everyone might not listen,
Some like maths, some like literacy
I will climb to reach my goals,
Beyond Year 5, we will open, grow and believe

Please show no rudeness,
To other people
As different as Year 5 and Year 4,
Make sure you climb to your goals before you fall.

Elsie Lindley (9)
Brooklands Farm Primary School, Milton Keynes

If I Ruled The World

If I ruled the world,
I would get rid of Burger King, vegetables, swear words
Also, bacteria and cigarettes

If I ruled the world,
Things I would change to make life easier,
Go on holiday every month, be happy,
Have lifts instead of stairs
And make Smiggle less expensive

If I ruled the world,
Things we just wouldn't have anymore,
School uniform, homeless people,
Coke, rudeness, cancer, Diet Coke and illness

If I ruled the world,
Things I would change from naughty,
Ice cream, pizza, cake, sweets
Cotton candy and midnight feasts.

Hannah Goodwin (8)
Brooklands Farm Primary School, Milton Keynes

If I Could Change The World

If I could change the world,
I would cancel school,
No bedtimes,
No gymnastics,
No cars

I would make football goals bigger,
I would make basketball goals forty-nine inches smaller
I would make there be no more arguments
There would be no more guns
There would be no bad dreams
The hours would be free

There would be no cancer,
No rich or poor people,
No violence
No landslides

I would make automatic cars
I would make sharks vegetarian

And for lions to be herbivores
I would make there be happiness in the world.

Logan Sewett (8)

Brooklands Farm Primary School, Milton Keynes

How To Be An Individual

Look at what we can achieve
It just happens when we believe
A relationship between you and me,
Shouldn't we be able to roam free?

We are all visible to see,
Some people just don't show jealousy
Some people are clever and don't need me,
I'm responsible and I'm also messy!

I'm helpful, clever and cheeky
I'm also friendly and happy
I don't like veggies,
But I like potato wedges

Listen to my worries please,
I pray for children to roam free
Every day I see a bee,
I just wish everyone had families.

Lucas Morris (9)
Brooklands Farm Primary School, Milton Keynes

Be The Individual I Want To See

Be the individual I want to see,
A better person I can be
A place my mistakes can roam free
Making me the student I can be

Listen to my talents please,
Who knows what I can achieve?
By opening my heart, I will succeed
It's possible, my brain believes

Sometimes my friends may not agree
Some like maths, others literacy
I will climb up my learning journey,
Beyond Year 5, my future I see

Please show no animosities,
To any race or minorities
As different as students from teachers,
A lonely foundation in a swarm of Year 3s.

Amelia Jefferson (9)

Brooklands Farm Primary School, Milton Keynes

If I Were In Charge Of The World

If I were in charge of the world,
I'd cancel detention, homework and studies,
Everyone would be equally smart and intelligent.

If I were in charge of the world,
Everyone would be rich and have friends,
Everything would be free, even iPads!

If I were in charge of the world,
You wouldn't have school,
And you wouldn't have Fortnite.

If I were in charge of the world,
A candy would be a vegetable,
And a person who forgets to brush their teeth,
Or sometimes forgets to have a bath,
Could still be in charge of the world.

Chahat Gurbani (8)

Brooklands Farm Primary School, Milton Keynes

Best Individual

Be the individual you want to see,
A better Year 5 for you and me,
A place our class can roam free,
Making me a successful learner.

Please tell me you will always be smiling,
Everyone will be happy when they're passing.
Don't forget your friends, of course,
Carry on like you're riding a horse.
We are sensible,
Don't forget to always be responsible.

Everyone may not agree,
Some like maths, others PE
Or work independently,
Just carry on your learning journey,
So be an individual, please,
That is my plea.

Austeja Poznanskaite (9)
Brooklands Farm Primary School, Milton Keynes

Be The Change I Want To See

Be the change I want to see,
A better school for you and me
A place my learning can roam free,
Making me as independent as I can be

Listen to my talents please,
Who knows what I will achieve?
By opening my heart, I will achieve,
It's possible, my brain believes

My friends may not agree,
Some like maths, others French
I will climb up my learning journey,
Beyond Year 5, my future I see

Please show more kindness,
To any race or minorities
As different as a pen from a pencil,
A lone girl in a swarm of boys.

Grace (9)
Brooklands Farm Primary School, Milton Keynes

Change

Everyone's worried,
Everything has changed,
But that's okay
Even if you're not with your best mates
It's time to say goodbye to old,
And let the new memories unfold

Everyone might not like change,
Others stay or shout, "Hooray!"
You may not run fast,
Or jump high
But you can do the best things,
You just have to try

As different as we might be,
We know we are amazing
When we open, grow, believe
The word will always stay in your life,
You thank it, even if it's tomorrow or tonight.

Lily-Grace Pink (9)
Brooklands Farm Primary School, Milton Keynes

If I Could Rule The World

If I could rule the world,
I would cancel schools
No landfills
No cars
No sweet potatoes

If I could change the world,
I would make football goals bigger
I would make basketball goals nine inches lower
I would ban girls
There would be unlimited food for everyone,
I would make more trees and plants

If I could rule the world,
I would stop war,
And unhappiness
I would give money to charity

If I could change the world,
I would change ice cream to fruit,
Crisps into vegetables and Coke into water.

Reyansh Totala (8)
Brooklands Farm Primary School, Milton Keynes

Be The Change I Want To See

Be the change I want to see,
A better person I can be
A place my freedom can roam free
Making me the individual I can be

Listen to my talents please,
Who knows what this verse believes?
By opening my heart, I will succeed
It's possible my brain achieves

My friends may not agree,
Some like dancing, others football
I will climb up my learning journey
Beyond Year 5, my future I see

Please show no rudeness,
To any race or year groups
As different as chalk from beans,
A lone wasp in a swarm of bees.

Tilly Locke (9)
Brooklands Farm Primary School, Milton Keynes

If I Were In Charge Of The World

If I were in charge of the world,
I'd get rid of cauliflower, guns, Fortnite and blood tests

If I were in charge of the world,
There'd be more homework, no prices or costs and longer-living people

If I were in charge of the world,
We wouldn't have bedtimes,
We would not have a lot of clothing stores,
And there'd be no such thing as laundry!

If I were in charge of the world,
Most unhealthy things would become healthy,
Even if someone forgot to flush or brush,
They could still be in charge of the world!

Nduka Jason C Okomba (9)
Brooklands Farm Primary School, Milton Keynes

If I Were In Charge Of The World

If I were in charge of the world,
I'd cancel school uniform, the boring music and
French

If I were in charge of the world,
Everything would be free,
Boys wouldn't be allowed at school
And no head teachers

If I were in charge of the world,
We wouldn't get homework, reading,
Teachers and boys could sit in the sewers with rats
on their heads

If I were in charge of the world,
You could have yoyos, hot chocolate,
Biscuits, sweets, chocolate, Fruit Winders,
Tea, coffee, Fruit Pastilles and protein bars.

Danielle Donovan (8)
Brooklands Farm Primary School, Milton Keynes

Be The Change You Want To See

Be the change you want to see,
A better person we will see
Make a school better for me,
Listen to my words please,
Who knows what this verse may achieve?
Will you be by my side,
And help me succeed?
My brain and yours have the power,
When we believe
People may not agree
Some people like to dance
Others like to sing
I would fly to the moon and back
For this world to be a better place
For you and me
Beyond the stars,
Love is what we see
Show the world,

Who we can be
Please be an individual.

Asia Nandoo (9)
Brooklands Farm Primary School, Milton Keynes

If I Were In Charge Of The World

If I were in charge of the world,
I'd cancel Fortnite, early mornings,
Raisins, school and teachers

If I were in charge of the world,
There'd be free things, no coffee,
No clocks and no eggs

If I were in charge of the world,
You wouldn't have horror movies,
You wouldn't have spiders
You wouldn't have bananas
You wouldn't even have homework

If I were in charge of the world,
I would change sweets and chocolate into
vegetables
Also, there would be no bullies, punching or
kicking!

Izzie Harvey (8)
Brooklands Farm Primary School, Milton Keynes

Make Your Changes

Be the change everyone wants to see,
A better place the world could be
A place where it's safe and everybody's smiley
Making Earth a nicer place to be

Listen to my heartbeat please,
Nobody knows what this verse achieves,
By far, our heart will always succeed
It's possible, my brain believes

Most of the others may not agree,
Some like cookies, others cream
I will manage to climb the highest branch of that
tree,
I will do it today,
I will do it tomorrow,
And every day, I achieve my dreams.

Kendra Evans (9)

Brooklands Farm Primary School, Milton Keynes

Be The Change You Always Dream

Be the change you always dream,
Amazing, strong, supportive you seem
Inside, you may feel really flappy
On the outside, you seem really happy

You and me need to be,
The key to unlock long living dreams
You can always rely on your friends
Life might seem to never end

Problems are not as bad as they seem,
When you use truth and honesty
Dance with your friends all day long,
Make sure that you dance to your favourite song

Please follow your dream,
Never forget how important they seem!

Zofia Natalia Pulido (9)
Brooklands Farm Primary School, Milton Keynes

Being An Individual

I n learning, always achieve

N ever let your wellbeing get low and think of 'open, grow and believe'

D on't fear, teachers are here and they will always help you succeed

I n learning zones, always believe and think of children in need

V ery energetic and I smile a lot

I am funny in a way

D on't hurry, stop your worry

U se your resources and be independent

A mazing learning, don't give up

L earn, learn always learn, give smiles and have fun.

Ellie Hyde (9)

Brooklands Farm Primary School, Milton Keynes

Every Time I Believe, I Achieve

Look at me, every time I believe, I achieve
All these things are not hard for me
Because I always achieve

No one is the same,
But we can all do the same
Especially each day

You will be a better person
To see and you will always achieve
And believe and you will be individual

You don't have to give up
Because we are determined
Believe, achieve
We are individual

Never give up because you have all your friends around you,
So you can always be individual.

Rory Sims (9)
Brooklands Farm Primary School, Milton Keynes

Change

Have you dreamt of a life full of change,
With a lifetime of happiness and change?
Everyone should have a chance to change,
Everyone should have a chance to be independent
When you change, it feels awesome
When you are independent, it feels great
Don't be afraid to change,
If you are with your friends, tell them
Today I am going to be an individual,
Change is good
Say hello to the new you
And say goodbye to the old you
This is you,
Don't be scared or afraid,
Change.

Dakota-Blue Young (10)

Brooklands Farm Primary School, Milton Keynes

If I Were In Charge Of The World

If I were in charge of the world,
I'd cancel brothers, sisters, detention and high
school

If I were in charge of the world,
There'd be no SATs, no school and no boys

If I were in charge of the world,
You wouldn't have Fortnite, football, head teachers
You wouldn't even have poems

If I were in charge of the world,
There would be no vegetables, fruit, behaviour
charts
People who ignored their parents
Would still be allowed to be in charge of the world.

Faith Ashington (8)
Brooklands Farm Primary School, Milton Keynes

Being Individual

I 'm always determined to complete my learning

N ever worry, teachers are there to help

D on't hurry, you have got people to support you

I 'm individual because I keep listening

V ery confident in my learning journey

I can be independent

D oing all I can to be individual

U se all resources in the classroom

A ll the children are here to support you

L earn, learn, learn, let's have fun in learning.

Aimee Nunn (9)

Brooklands Farm Primary School, Milton Keynes

Individual Change

Be the individual you can be,
Doing the things that you can do.
If everybody changes clearly through,
The world will be a better place.

To change the world, change yourself first,
Be a role model and make others change.
Soon, you'll notice that the world has changed,
To a better world, an individual world.

Individuals don't need other people,
They know what they need to do.
Changing into an individual is hard,
But trust me, it's great.

Tristan Law (9)
Brooklands Farm Primary School, Milton Keynes

Be The Individual You Want To Be

Be the change we all want to see,
A better Year 5 learner I can be,
A place my skills can roam free,
Making me the best person who will succeed.

Listen to my learning please,
Who knows what the next verse can achieve?
By believing in myself, I will succeed,
It's possible, my heart believes.

My teachers and friends may not agree,
Some like literacy,
I will climb my individual journey,
Beyond Year 5,
My Brooklands future, I see.

Amielia Caroline Kay (10)
Brooklands Farm Primary School, Milton Keynes

If I Ruled Earth

If I ruled Earth,
I would get rid of cancer,
Cigarettes, illness, school dinners
And Fortnite

If I ruled Earth,
I would have my own stationery,
Mansion, bigger bedrooms,
And unicorn

If I ruled Earth,
I wouldn't have meat,
I'd meet my friends every day,
And everyone would be neat

If I ruled Earth,
Fruit would be chocolate,
Vegetables would be reading,
And school would be a trampoline park.

Ezra Sana Hashemi (9)
Brooklands Farm Primary School, Milton Keynes

Individual

I ndividuality is the key

N eat as can be

D own and up, the handwriting pen goes

I n my lovely book

"V ery good," the teacher said with a smile

I am an individual learner now

D ance the whole night long

"U se your fantastic brain," said my friend

'A BC', I wrote in my book

"L ook at this," the teacher said, "read it to the class."

Jaime Cross (9)

Brooklands Farm Primary School, Milton Keynes

This Is Me!

This is me, all individual, you see?
I believe you want to see how amazing I can be
My skills are good,
I'm kind and caring
I'm like the change the world might need

Friendship is the key,
Achieve resembles me
This is why learning is meant for me,
To be the best I can be

I have an open heart,
An open mindset
And most important of all
I believe
And this is why I'm individual, you see?

Selin Kocum (9)
Brooklands Farm Primary School, Milton Keynes

Individuals

I ndividuals can easily believe
N umber ones can achieve
D espite anyone else's religion
I ndependent is the best decision
V ery many people take the test
I n your heart, you are the best
D o you see what I see?
U s, you, me, independent is what to be
A ll day, every day, be amazing
L earning journeys will keep on rising,
S o be an individual!

Erin Ebrahim (9)

Brooklands Farm Primary School, Milton Keynes

Be The Individual I Want To Be

Be the change I want to see,
A better learner I can be
A place my talents can roam free,
Marking me as individual

Listen to my talents please,
Who knows what this environment achieves?
By opening, growing and believing, I will succeed,
It's possible, my brain believes

My community may not agree,
Some like learning, others PE
I will take big steps on my journey,
Beyond Year 5, my future.

Ruby Chambers (9)
Brooklands Farm Primary School, Milton Keynes

The Changes I Can See

Be the change I want to see,
A better person I can be,
A place my personality can roam free,
Making me the individual I can be.

Listen to my talent please,
Who knows what this world can be?
By growing my learning I will succeed,
It's possible, my heart believes.

My classmates may not agree,
Some like maths, others PE,
I will weave my learning journey,
In Year 5, you'll see a new me.

Aleena Farooqui (10)
Brooklands Farm Primary School, Milton Keynes

If I Were In Charge Of The World

If I were in charge of the world,
I'd cancel detentions,
School homework
Alarm clocks and teachers

If I were in charge of the world,
There'd be everything for free,
No tutors and French

If I were in charge of the world,
You wouldn't have a behaviour chart,
You wouldn't have injections
You wouldn't have rulers
Or healthy food
You wouldn't even have clocks.

Hamsini Bacchu (8)
Brooklands Farm Primary School, Milton Keynes

Individual

Be the individual you want to be,
A better school for you and me
Where learning journeys can roam free
Make things how they used to be

Listen to my ambitions please,
Who knows what my work achieves?
For great work my book it needs,
It's possible, my brain believes

Everyone may not agree,
Some like maths, others PE
Some group A, B or C
Beyond the work, more work they see.

Dalitso Mpepo (10)
Brooklands Farm Primary School, Milton Keynes

If I Were In Charge Of The World

If I were in charge of the world,
I'd cancel school days and old parks

If I were in charge of the world,
I would make it into a Fortnite world
Because everyone loves it!

If I were in charge of the world,
I wouldn't have teachers

If I were in charge of the world,
I wouldn't have baby stuff

If I were in charge of the world,
I wouldn't have cricket.

Muhammad Hassan Maher (8)
Brooklands Farm Primary School, Milton Keynes

Individuals

I ndividuals can achieve
N umber ones can believe in anything
D ependable as you see
I n this world, we can be free
V ery much, people believe in me
I n your heart, you can succeed
D etermined as you can be
U sing my advice, you can achieve
A nd my poet's love, you can believe
L earning is so important for your education.

Sandra Sreekumar (9)
Brooklands Farm Primary School, Milton Keynes

Jeff The Evil Roomba

Jeff the Evil Roomba was different from the rest,
He went to fight Testificate Man to prove he was the best
Fight he might but he lost this war,
Testificate Man... he was just more

When he came back,
He had a great pack
But now in his reality,
They were proving their individuality

In the end,
He found a friend
He was finally free,
To be the best he could be!

Asher Peter Buluku Roberts (10)

Brooklands Farm Primary School, Milton Keynes

If I Ruled The Planet

If I ruled the planet,
I'd cancel murder and cancer.

If I ruled the planet,
There'd be unlimited food for everyone,
Sweets instead of vegetables,
Chocolate instead of fruit.

If I ruled the planet,
You wouldn't have bedtimes
You wouldn't have dinner
You wouldn't have baths
And sharks wouldn't hurt humans
When they ride on a boat!

Megan Brooke Denehan (9)
Brooklands Farm Primary School, Milton Keynes

Individuals

I ndividuals can always achieve
N umber ones believe in everyone
D etermined people always succeed
I n the world, we always succeed
V ery many people believe in me
I n your heart, you can achieve
D ifferent people have different ideas
U sing my advice, you can do it too
A lways listen to others
L earn more every day.

Rachel Grunwell (9)
Brooklands Farm Primary School, Milton Keynes

Individual

I 'm unique

N ever give up, even when things are tricky

D inosaurs are cool, I love them

I like my Xbox because it's fun and engaging

V ery loud and crazy

I ncredible goalie saving all the goals

D etermined to achieve

U nbelievably good at making friends

A cheeky person making others laugh

L iking everyone.

Mason Woolf (9)

Brooklands Farm Primary School, Milton Keynes

If I Was Queen

If I was queen,
I would get rid of poverty,
Sadness, bacteria and bedtimes.

If I was queen,
To make life easier, I would add happy families,
More books, more money and more art.

If I was queen,
I wouldn't have any more rudeness, swearing,
Fortnite and snow.

If I was queen,
Homework, ice cream and sweets
Would change from being unhealthy to good.

Jenai Allison (8)
Brooklands Farm Primary School, Milton Keynes

Individual

Open,
Grow,
Believe
Means we will all achieve
I believe this is the key to succeed

We have to go through many stages,
Which sometimes feels like ages

Listen to me please,
Sometimes mistakes can roam free

It's possible, my heart believes,
Everyone can achieve

Listen to my worries please,
It does take a lot of believing
And achieving.

Daisy Lowen (9)
Brooklands Farm Primary School, Milton Keynes

If I Were In Charge Of The World

If I were in charge of the world,
I'd cancel school, homework and detentions

If I were in charge of the world,
I would make there be more football,
And less sugar in sweets

If I were in charge of the world,
You would have more money,
You would have more football

If I were in charge of the world,
I would get rid of teachers, schools and zoos.

Kayhan Moradi (8)
Brooklands Farm Primary School, Milton Keynes

If I Ruled The World

If I ruled the world,
I would cancel gunshots and murder
If I ruled the world
I would cancel cancer and illness

If I ruled the world,
Jam tarts, chocolate and sweets would be
vegetables
If I ruled the world,
Everything would be voice-activated

If I ruled the world,
Everything would be 1p

If I ruled the world,
I'd cancel pain.

Jack Morris (8)
Brooklands Farm Primary School, Milton Keynes

If I Were In Charge Of The World

If I were in charge of the world,
I'd cancel Fortnite
All year and month,
All day, TV and iPads are playing

If I were in charge of the world,
There would be no football,
A robot flying into space,
Trap doors all over the world

If I were in charge of the world,
Chocolate would be a vegetable,
Basketball,
Monkey bars would be a sport!

Michael Sagar (8)
Brooklands Farm Primary School, Milton Keynes

The Right Individual

Be the change you want to see,
A better school for you and me
We are responsible,
We are who we are
We have the rights
Let's hold them tight

I can, you can, we all can

Everyone may not agree,
Individuality is a place to achieve
Don't be ashamed,
We are all the same
Always stay connected,
It's the key to friendship.

Dhioni Tailor (9)
Brooklands Farm Primary School, Milton Keynes

An Individual

Be the person you want to see,
Not a twin that you don't want to be
A place for our freedom to come alive,
Not a hellish place where your spirits can't survive

Be individual, let yourself thrive,
Go to a place where your angels can revive
Drop your worries,
Go roam free!
We know that you will succeed,
Go on, go and achieve!

Leon Moradi (9)
Brooklands Farm Primary School, Milton Keynes

Seasons

C hristmas is a season when it snows
H alloween is a season when you go out at night trick or treating
A utumn comes after spring and leaves fall off lots of trees!
N ovember is a month when it starts to snow
G reat seasons happen throughout the year
E aster is a season when the Easter bunny comes and hides eggs.

Skye Jessica Astle (7)

Brooklands Farm Primary School, Milton Keynes

Celebration

C hristmas is a celebration in winter

H alloween is a scary holiday that you can dress up for

A utumn is a season in which leaves fall

N ovember is the day that a new month starts

G reat seasons are here, give them a cheer!

E aster is the season that the Easter bunny comes to your house and hides chocolate eggs.

Ameya Polavajram (7)

Brooklands Farm Primary School, Milton Keynes

Change About Growing Up

C hildren start off as babies
H aving to work at primary school
A ll teenagers go to high school
N ow teenagers are going to university
G rowing up and having your own responsibility
E very second you learn and grow and get better and change. You change your life and change the world.

Annabella Okafor (7)

Brooklands Farm Primary School, Milton Keynes

Individual

I am independent

N ever give up

D etermined to achieve

I ncredible at football

V ery kind and helpful

I am a good friend

D oing the right things

U nique forever

A mazing school, this place is

L ove your time here because it will whizz!

Jake Coxhill (9)

Brooklands Farm Primary School, Milton Keynes

Seasons

C hristmas is a popular celebration in winter
H alloween is a spooky, scary celebration in autumn
A utumn is a season when all the leaves fall off the trees
N aughty seasons are winter and summer
G reat changes can happen in lovely seasons
E very day is the best in all seasons.

Erin Spensley (7)

Brooklands Farm Primary School, Milton Keynes

Growing Up

C hildren learn to walk and talk
H umans that are toddlers can walk but they
  can't talk
A ny child can walk and talk perfectly
N ow, when I am a teenager, I will go to university
G rown-ups do work every single day
E lderly people sometimes do knitting and lots of
  cooking.

Anaya Umer (7)
Brooklands Farm Primary School, Milton Keynes

The Perfect Individual

What a perfect individual is,
They can get their work done in a whizz.
How they work is outstanding,
If you give it a try you might succeed.

Now listen to my ideas please,
Now you can be an individual and achieve.
Organised individuals are lovely and talented,
You should try now and achieve.

Isabella Purdy-Cross (9)

Brooklands Farm Primary School, Milton Keynes

Be The Best Individual You Can Be

Be the perfect individual you can be,
A change from easy to hard
A world where individuals roam free

A place where people achieve,
Everyone is different
One may like science,
Others geography
Don't convince them, it's their opinion
So make a change for once and for all.

Hrithvik Daggu (9)

Brooklands Farm Primary School, Milton Keynes

Seasons

C hristmas is in a snowy season and then it changes to summer

H ollow trees grow in summer and die in autumn

A utumn has lots of colourful, crunchy leaves!

N ew Year's Eve is in winter

G reat things happen when change takes over

E aster comes in spring.

Shannon Lavery-Singh (7)

Brooklands Farm Primary School, Milton Keynes

Caterpillar To Butterfly

C aterpillar curls when it is big and strong to be a butterfly

H as to change to its beautiful wings and colours

A ppetite is big when leaves are all over the trees

N ever wants to be the same

G ets ready to jump into a cocoon

E ager to fly.

Isla Lloyd (7)

Brooklands Farm Primary School, Milton Keynes

Growing Up

C hildren learn to get dressed to go to school
H umans are different to puppies, humans can talk to you
A teenager is different to a baby
N annies have wrinkly skin
G randmas are very kind
E ven they love each other in their family.

Hattie Hughes- Stone (7)

Brooklands Farm Primary School, Milton Keynes

Rainbow

R ed is bright, dark, pretty or dull
A lligators are bright green
I gloos are really white
N ice colours make me happy
B right colours make my eyes hurt
O ctopuses are orange and I like orange
W hales are dark blue.

Emilia Kendall (8)

Brooklands Farm Primary School, Milton Keynes

Caterpillars

C aterpillars start from cocoons
H unting food makes them grow up
A butterfly can fly really high in the sky
N o butterfly can go back to a caterpillar
G etting ready for a butterfly is easy
E nding being a big butterfly.

Olivia Zajkowska (7)

Brooklands Farm Primary School, Milton Keynes

New Changes

Changes may be scary,
So don't go all wary
When you win, you go, "Hooray!"
But learning for today
Learning is my hobby,
Doing it makes me happy
I am legendary
But also very crazy
Being friendly,
Is better than being silly.

Mathys Levet (9)
Brooklands Farm Primary School, Milton Keynes

Seasons

S end different weather
E very day the trees change
A mazing weather
S tay the same for three months
O n the way to a whole new season
N ot every year is it the same
S o not every time it's the same.

Niamh Carrington (7)
Brooklands Farm Primary School, Milton Keynes

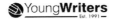

My Big Change

My mum has cancer,
She is not well
I have got to help her day and night
Sometimes it is hard
So I write her a little card
When she is ill,
I give her a pill
So that's my poem,
So now I've shared mine,
What's yours?

Amelie (7)
Brooklands Farm Primary School, Milton Keynes

Change

C hanges can be good and bad
H ard changes are difficult to choose from
A hard change is bad
N o changes can be miserable
G o and make a good change
E ars are good for listening to new teachers.

Alfie James Gordon (7)
Brooklands Farm Primary School, Milton Keynes

Weather

W et water
E very day, the weather changes
A lways summery and hot
T hunder
H orrendous weather
E mergency in summer for whales
R ain is good for the grass
S un.

Callan Lindsay (7)
Brooklands Farm Primary School, Milton Keynes

Growing Up

C hildren learn, children talk
H urrying to grow up first
A nd when I was a baby, I was tiny
N ow that I am big, I am tall
G rowing up is fun
E ven if I fall, I will get back up.

Eve Gallagher (7)
Brooklands Farm Primary School, Milton Keynes

See The Change In You

Be the best you can be,
See the change that you are going to be,
Recreate yourself,
Be the person that you want to be.

Free your spirit,
Free your heart,
Free your mind,
And don't look behind.

Theo M Salifu (9)

Brooklands Farm Primary School, Milton Keynes

My Poems

When I was one, I had some fun,
When I was two, I ate some stew
As I grew, I learnt to walk and talk,
And talk and talk and talk!
When I turned five, I gave high fives
When I'm twenty, I'll work and get plenty.

Grace French (7)

Brooklands Farm Primary School, Milton Keynes

Change

C hange your actions to be nice
H ave a positive mind during change
A nything can happen in a change
N o one is the same
G reat things can happen in change
E njoy your change.

Alfie Sanderson (7)
Brooklands Farm Primary School, Milton Keynes

Firework

F ireworks can change colour
I n the sky
R ed and orange
E ver moving
W ill it land?
O oh, it's lovely
R ocket into space
K eeping eyes open wide.

Isabella Derham (7)

Brooklands Farm Primary School, Milton Keynes

If I Were King Of The World

If I were king of the world, I would cancel guns
If I were king of the world, I would cancel cancer
If I were king of the world, I would cancel knives
If I were king of the world, I would cancel bullies.

Taylor Dunn (9)
Brooklands Farm Primary School, Milton Keynes

The Butterfly

B aby born
U tterly pretty
T otally amazing
T errifying, not!
E nvironment
R epresent life
F ly
L ive
Y oung and old.

Bella Pringle (7)

Brooklands Farm Primary School, Milton Keynes

Change

C hange your actions
H ave an amazing attitude
A nybody can change
N obody is bad for changing
G row into a better person
E njoy changes!

Kai Buckley (7)
Brooklands Farm Primary School, Milton Keynes

Jack And The Dragon's Adventure

I am Jack, I am a quarterback
My pet's name is Waggon, he's a baby dragon
Me and Waggon had a dream,
To make a movie, space was the theme
Earlier, NASA invited me to space,
My heart was beating at a fast pace
Me and my friends had a card game race,
I had a joker and the diamond ace
I jumped out the rocket,
With my hand in my pocket
Waggon followed, he made a sound
It went *bing bong!* He roared out loud
We saw Pluto and then Mars
I returned to the rocket in the shape of cars,
When I got home, my mum was mad
I was chased towards my dad
They shouted, "Where, oh where have you both been?"
I answered back, "You won't guess what I've seen!"

Jamie Saunders (10)
Giffard Park Primary School, Giffard Park

Superbaby

Superbaby,
Little and strong
Popped out the mother
And was as strong as King Kong!

With a six pack as hard as rock,
He was buff and fast
When the nurses came in,
They gave a big gasp

A cry came out the window
With a horrid punch
The baby turned around,
With a thought that someone was for lunch!

Superbaby flew out the window,
Past a woman big for her size
When he got out of the hospital,
There was a nasty surprise...

Two men beating an old lady
Looked up to see the flying baby

They screamed at the sight that met their eyes
Superbaby went to give them a piece of his mind

He punched, he kicked
While getting kicked by shoes
He pulled down the trousers of one of the men
The guy with the trousers pulled down was
wearing knickers!

Samuel Inwood (10)

Giffard Park Primary School, Giffard Park

The Day The Cookies Took Over The World

The day the cookies took over the world,
It wasn't a very good day
The day the cookies took over the world,
I thought it was just a game
The day the cookies took over the world,
I thought they wanted to play
The day the cookies took over the world,
I didn't know what to say
The day the cookies took over the world,
I was very afraid
The day the cookies took over the world,
They told us what to say
The day the cookies took over the world,
So there was no time to waste
The day the cookies took over the world,
The adults didn't know what to do
The day the cookies took over the world,
I came up with a plan
I doused them with milk,

They all fell apart,
The day the cookies took over.

Talitha Grace Mkwashi (10)
Giffard Park Primary School, Giffard Park

A Girl With A Hair Styling Comb

There was once a girl who had a dream,
A dream about a chocolate stream
She had a magic comb,
Which made her hair look like a dome
Then she moved to Candyland
Where dome hair was banned
So she threw away her comb,
And said, "Bye-bye, dome!"
She walked in the woods, past talking trees,
Then she saw chocolate bees
She grabbed one from the sky,
Then she realised it was hard to fly
She started to plummet to the ground,
How could she ever be found?
Suddenly, Prince Charming came
The girl thought he was totally lame
He caught her, she said, "Thank you!"
Even though he wasn't her boo

Then she shouted, "I miss my hair dome!"
And then she moved back home.

Grace Ellery (11)

Giffard Park Primary School, Giffard Park

A Flying Horse?

There once was a horse,
A weird one to be precise
All the horses stared
At this very pretty sight
But then the horses got confused
As to why, upon this horse's head, lay a cone
Was there any other horse like this?
Or was she on her own?
Then the horses saw
This weird horse start to fly
Was this a dream or reality?
Somebody please tell them why!
Up above the clouds, the crystal blue sky
She kept on coming and coming,
Was this truth or a lie?
Sparkly, fluffy clouds
Magical, mystical indeed
Cute, fluffy and amazeballs
But as the horses just stared
The thing above the horse's head wasn't a cone,
It was a horn

Could it be real?
A horse or a unicorn?

Rebecca Gill (11)
Giffard Park Primary School, Giffard Park

The Disaster With The Goat And The Glue Sticks

I woke up,
What a dream, I thought
A goat that I had bought
Terrified, I scrambled out of bed,
Nearly hitting my head!
I walked out to the fields,
I trampled on something
With a *ding, bing* and a *ting!*
A field full of glue sticks
"How unusual!" I cried
"How great for my class!"
Turning around because of the sound
Horror filled me within
This creature had wings,
And eyes that filled me with dread
It took me aboard
I was riding a goat
I screamed and shouted
I couldn't stop

But before I knew it,
I was down in a shock
Back in my bed at home.

Francesca Jane Sicorello (11)
Giffard Park Primary School, Giffard Park

Greedy Acrobats

There is a circus on the beach,
The ringmaster slipped on some bleach
The bleach was made out of kelp,
The acrobats came to help
The elephants made a noise,
The acrobats put down their toys
The acrobats ran
They were running as fast as a van
The elephants saw their black costumes
They had gone back to their dressing rooms
The elephants found them
They had made a little den
The elephants were eaten by the acrobats
All that was left were the elephant hats
The ringmaster began to sigh
He needed a new act and they were the reason why
Last week, they ate the lions too,
Who would be next? It could be you!

Grace Black (10)
Giffard Park Primary School, Giffard Park

My Hairy, Farting Foot

I have a hairy foot,
A hairy foot that farts
Every time I take a step,
Everybody laughs

People keep on saying that my name is Stink
Bomb,
They don't even care that my real name is Tom
As I walk down the street,
Everyone stares at my stinky feet
I feel so embarrassed as I have no shoes,
But oh well, what have I got to lose?

I have a hairy foot,
A hairy foot that farts
Every time I take a step,
Everybody laughs

I go to work, it's not much
I also have a dog that nobody will touch
People say I'm foul and ugly
But I don't really care because this is me!

Elain Krayem (11)
Giffard Park Primary School, Giffard Park

Horrid Burping Board

The burping board, as rude as can be
He's always trying to frame me
It was just another boring day at school
When my teacher went to go and get some writing tools
Then the board blinked,
It burped and it winked
I looked at the board as it burped and wrote, "Billy was here!"
The head teacher walked in and said, "Oh dear!"
From the corner of my eye,
It was extremely sly
As my teacher walked through the door
She screamed and said, "Oh my, is that manure?"
"Billy, detention! Detention for you!"
But it wasn't my fault, the board drew a picture of poo!

Ella Glass (10)

Giffard Park Primary School, Giffard Park

The Argument Of The Cheese And Crackers

Cheese and crackers hate each other
Like a sister and a brother
Always arguing, it isn't right
They just have to forever fight
"Hey, Cracker, you're so dry,
No one can deny
We will never work together,
Just stay away forever!"
"No, no, Cheese, you're wrong,
Eww, you really pong!
All day you sit on my nose,
Maybe you should change your pose..."
Suddenly, Saint Knife is here,
"Guys, don't fear,
I'll save the day!
Then we can shout hooray!"
He stacks crackers with cheese,
And now this is a snack that will please.

Emily Gunn (10)
Giffard Park Primary School, Giffard Park

The Megalodon Pop!

One day, I went to the moon,
I saw a megalodon on a balloon!
He was gold, bold
And very old
And five minutes later,
There was a man who was a hater
He was shouting and screaming
I thought, *I must be dreaming!*
He travelled to the moon,
To pop the balloon
He shot and shot until he hit,
I started a fire, the balloon was lit
The megalodon fell with ease
He realised he was being teased,
The man got angry, he got mad
The megalodon was very, very sad
He asked, "Can't you stay?"
The man said, "I hate balloons!"
And went away.

Kacper Oskar Zak (10)
Giffard Park Primary School, Giffard Park

Chips That Rob

Did you know chips can rob you?
When you sleep
Chips wake up, then do their make-up
They colour themselves black and white
And try not to wake you up in a fright
They sneak around in groups of three,
As you wake up to go for a wee wee
Right behind them is a trail of grease
Because they're the worst robbers since baked
beans

They don't rob for normal things, oh no
They rob for barbecue sauce, ketchup and even
mayo
Before you wake up, they sneak right out
Then they start to think about what they will do
If in the kitchen, they run to you.

Jamie Windebank (10)
Giffard Park Primary School, Giffard Park

Rubby-Man's Shoplifting Adventure

As soon as I was eight years old,
I went to the shop to buy something cold,
I then saw Rubby-Man, but he was blue,
He looked as though he needed the loo,
He grabbed an apple, he grabbed a pear,
He even grabbed someone's hair,
He looked at the doors and started to hop,
One minute later, he was out of the shop!
As quick as lightning, he was down the street,
He looked around for something to eat,
He ran fast, right to his house,
As quickly and quietly as a mouse,
He stayed in his house forever and ever,
Rubby-Man left his house, never, never!

Chloe Brown (10)
Giffard Park Primary School, Giffard Park

The Day The Disco Ball Took Over

The day the disco ball took over,
I didn't know what to do
The day the disco ball took over,
I was in a panic
The day the disco ball took over,
My dad was playing a game
The day the disco ball took over,
My mum was getting the blame
The day the disco ball took over,
My brother wasn't at home
The day the disco ball took over,
My sister was all alone
The day the disco ball took over,
We were all afraid
It made us all dance,
It made us all laugh
And it even made us scream
The day the disco ball took over.

Sahl Fowzulameen (10)
Giffard Park Primary School, Giffard Park

On My Trip To The Moon

On my trip to the moon, I will take...
A hair from a unicorn
Three spotty, mouldy mushrooms from a witch's bungalow
And a picture of a waterfall made of chocolate

On my trip to the moon, I will eat...
Rainbow spaghetti with cloud fluff
Elf ice cream with fairy sauce
And gummy bear soup with a candyfloss roll

On my trip to the moon, I will see...
Sharks swimming in asteroid belts
Stars dancing the Macarena
And a city where pink Martians tap dance all day!

On my trip to the moon, I will have so much fun!

Jasmine Charlotte Wareing (10)

Giffard Park Primary School, Giffard Park

Blind Cat Food

Blind cat food singing opera,
Eardrums were popping like bubbles
The smells were disgusting like vomit
People were running from the town hall
The smell was making people say, "Eww!"

The town hall was collapsing
But the cat food couldn't see a thing
And couldn't hear anything
When it fell to the ground,
The cat food survived

Unfortunately, the police arrived,
And when the blind cat food arrived
The security and inmates went to the toilet
Then the cat food made eardrums pop!

Dragos Mihai Pascu (10)
Giffard Park Primary School, Giffard Park

Flying Foam Strawberries

I was surprised to see, the other day
Bright pink, foam strawberries flying my way
They looked delicious
Though they seemed suspicious
I tried to catch one, they were too quick
I tried again with a Sellotape-covered stick
Finally, I grabbed one, it tried to get free
But I shoved it in my mouth so very quickly
The next thing I knew, I'd spat it out
It was disgusting, plus it had started to shout!
I would never eat one again,
I vowed on that day
I'll stick to flying apples and bananas maybe!

Jessica Asumbwe (10)
Giffard Park Primary School, Giffard Park

Chocolate Cheetahs Playing Hide-And-Seek

There are chocolate cheetahs playing hide-and-seek,
Hey! Hey! Don't you peek!
Quick, let's go and join the fun,
The winner's been promised a jam-filled bun!

Look, there's a hiding place underneath the slide,
Let's just hope no one goes for a ride!
A cheetah's hiding behind a tree
Oh no! He's just been stung by a bee!

Now the sun's coming out,
This means the cheetahs are going to melt!
I lick my lips and begin to run,
Then I realise I have won!

Alicia Faid (11)
Giffard Park Primary School, Giffard Park

The Gruesome Ghost Of Number Thirteen

N ever go to house number thirteen
U nless you want to be scared
M ind out for the spookies
B e careful because
E ven when you have a torch
R onald the tickle skeleton is going to get you

T here are spindly spiders
H iggledy-piggledy trolls
I nvisible men
R eady to jump
T urn back before you get scared!
E ager to jump
E ager to scare
N ever go to number thirteen.

Finley Wirth (10)
Giffard Park Primary School, Giffard Park

When Animals Changed Colour

It was a beautiful day,
So I shouted, "Hooray!"
I wanted to see the unicorns,
With their pretty horns
When I saw them, they were blue
So I thought they had the flu
I checked on the other animals
To see if they had it too
Then I checked the bunnies,
In case they weren't good
They had changed too,
They were all green
They had changed overnight
They all seemed happy,
They all seemed fine
So I left them as they were alright.

Grace Lillie Mundye (11)
Giffard Park Primary School, Giffard Park

Trapped In A Clock With A Cat

I chased the cat around the room,
We came across the grandfather clock
As we stared, I felt a pull
So grabbed the cat as it sucked us in
All we heard was *tick-tock*,
From all the clocks around
I was terrified
Grandfather clocks, pocket watches,
Alarm clocks and digital clocks
It was like a little clock village
I could see a glimpse of light
All around us
Numbers surrounded us
I was terrified,
I didn't believe what I was seeing.

Ella Angell (10)
Giffard Park Primary School, Giffard Park

146

Standing On A Moon Made Of Cheese

In the middle of space,
Where there's a tangy, cheesy taste
I stood on the cheesy moon
The massive cheesy moon was colossal compared to my balloon!
The cheese was yummy and soft,
Even though it was as dark as your loft.
As I saw a quarter of the moon missing,
I saw a small, weird thing,
It must have been an alien,
It also could have been an Italian!
Oh no, the planet burger crashed
Into the cheese moon,
Which made a cheeseburger planet!

Rory McCauley (10)

Giffard Park Primary School, Giffard Park

The Horrid, Flossing Foot

The horrid flossing foot,
Knows how to cook
But doesn't know how to wash
He was in the war,
Got hit by a door
And now he is flossing on the floor,
That horrid, flossing foot

The horrid, flossing foot,
As sweaty as can be
Unfortunately, he got flattened by a tree
And he started calling his mummy
Shouting, "I'm so dirty, itchy and hairy!
Mummy, help me!"
That horrid, flossing foot.

Jack Harry Lawson (10)
Giffard Park Primary School, Giffard Park

The Tiny Chips Flossing

Tiny chips flossing
As hard as can be
In the little box of chips
As happy as can be

The small face,
On the tiny little red pot
Being cheeky by winking to the worker,
Small, active arms flossing speedily

Bright yellow chips,
Uneaten just like me
Small active arms,
Cool like me

Frying long chips
Waiting to be served
In a small little pot,
Crying to be heard.

Amber Hussain (10)
Giffard Park Primary School, Giffard Park

Down The Drain To Food Land

I play with my pig around the room,
Around the room we go
Around the room I find a drain
And down the drain we go
Down the drain I smell a smell,
A horrid smell from below

From below I see a sight
A sight of a magical land
In the land, I see some sweets
I see some sweets above the clouds
So above the clouds I go
Above the clouds, I see the sun
And my pig starts chasing the sun.

Tabitha Hancock (10)
Giffard Park Primary School, Giffard Park

A Glittery Mop Cleaning Pluto

I once got a telescope for my birthday
I built it, then I looked out of it,
I saw something going around in circles
It had glitter coming out of it,
It looked like a mop!
So I booked a flight to this mysterious light
And went to have a look at this delight
It felt so smooth and looked spotless
It was cleaning the sparkle from the stars
But there was something else,
It was cleaning out the gunk.

Toby Jarvis (10)
Giffard Park Primary School, Giffard Park

Biscuit Surfing

One fine evening, I saw something strange
There was a brown, soggy shape in the ocean
It started to come towards me,
A dog biscuit on a log!
The dog biscuit slashed me,
All I could taste was sea salt
It waved, it jumped, it half-piped
I laughed, I pointed, I smiled
Then all of a sudden, a jelly sea dog appeared
He snaffled that surfing biscuit down in one
I cried, I wailed, then I went to bed!

Alfie James Ray (10)
Giffard Park Primary School, Giffard Park

My Shopping Spree

While I was out shopping, something made me smile,
Furniture was dancing down the aisle
Tables were tangoing with the chairs
Whilst the sofas were cha-chaing, catching the lamps unawares

In the meantime, the wardrobes were waltzing with the doors
In the distance, desks were sambaing across the floors
I'd only gone shopping to buy some sweets,
But the furniture dancing was a better treat!

Jack Mitchell (10)
Giffard Park Primary School, Giffard Park

A Disco In The Clouds

As I flew up through the clouds,
Feeling rather proud
I saw something quite bizarre
Looking at me from afar
I saw a disco ball floating,
I thought, *I must be dreaming*
Then a disco floor appeared
I looked around and found a dancing crow
And a prancing owl and even an ostrich or two
I thought, *I should join them and have a dance*,
As they were having a blast!

Alfie King (11)
Giffard Park Primary School, Giffard Park

My Cherries

My name is Mary and I'm buying my cherries
I thought about chocolate but then I chose
cherries
But something extraordinary happened to me
I was hit in the face by a big, hairy pea!
He came up so close and I couldn't see
And then he blinded me
The pea ran away but now where are my cherries?
They're gone, my cherries,
They're squished by the hairy pea!

Katie Hawes (11)
Giffard Park Primary School, Giffard Park

The Crazy Farting Fridge

I have a crazy fridge, so crazy that it farts
And made a secret base full of gas masks
So every time my fridge farts, I don't know where to start
I once opened the fridge and found a giraffe doing yoga
Until I noticed at the corner,
A llama giving praise and honour
"What?" I cried out
And that's the story of the farting fridge.

Shammah Doka (11)
Giffard Park Primary School, Giffard Park

The Day There Were No More Trees

It was such a beautiful day,
The sun was bright,
The grass was green,
But there were no trees in sight
I looked out the window,
And saw the trees holding bags
Oh no! They were going away
What could I do?
This was a disaster!
How were we going to breathe?
No flowers, no plants, no trees!
What kind of world was this?

Nadina Satala (10)

Giffard Park Primary School, Giffard Park

Drinking Water From The Cloud

An ordinary day and an ordinary life,
All I see is clouds
That everyone sees
But today wasn't one of those days
All clouds came down
All down to town
They were melting because of the sun
That was sunbathing
The clouds turned into water,
"Why don't we drink it?"

Jacquiline Badu (10)
Giffard Park Primary School, Giffard Park

Once Upon A Snowman

I was walking through the wicked wood,
But what did I turn back to find?
Snow-covered trees, snow people everywhere
But they looked kind

They wore red and white scarves,
Some even had black coats
Bobble hats on their heads,
And some arrived on boats

I was shivering cold, dressed for summer,
Not for sleeping in an igloo!
No coat, no hat, just woolly socks
Mum had insisted, like mums always do!

The snowmen greeted my kindly,
They said, "Come over here and join the fun run,
It's only once a year!"

A booming voice on a megaphone shouted,
"Contestants to the start line!"
We all jogged over and
I just hoped it would work out fine!

Anna L
Hughenden Primary School, Hughenden Valley

My Friend Is A Giant

A giant that walks,
A giant that talks
One that loves hopscotch,
But I love hopscotch too
The giant that has been all over the news
I know where he lives
But I won't tell you, it's a secret
Even though he is bigger than me
When he's sleeping, I'm in my room
I hear talking but no one's there, only books
I go and check and it's the books
When I want to play with him, he turns into an ant
When he doesn't, he gets bigger again
He has a genie for a pet and once gave me lots of
wishes
I wished for an adventure
He gave me one to visit the clouds,
That's how the giant's my best friend.

Emily Read (10)
Ivingswood Academy, Greenway

Rainbow-Eating Monsters

They live in a computer game,
Llamacorns are their names
They play all day,
Then hide away

When they come out,
They play and shout
Looking for rainbows to eat
They look around searching the ground,
Like bloodthirsty hounds

When they find a rainbow,
They shout with glee
And say, "Tee hee hee!"

Then they eat the rainbow,
They gobble it up
Finish it off,
Then run back to Retail Row.

Tayla Stanley (10)
Ivingswood Academy, Greenway

Helping A Dragon

When I brush his teeth,
I think of smelly feet
When I look at the ground,
I say, "Don't growl!"
When I see meat out of his mouth,
I think, *ew, that's a disgusting sound!*
When I put the brush down,
There's a horrible sound!
When the bees hum,
I think, *what have I done?*
When I think of the six times table,
I begin to itch
Then when I sit down,
I begin to stay down.

Bilal Jarcheh (10)
Ivingswood Academy, Greenway

Fearful Ladybird

Once a ladybird sang,
Then it saw a dragon's terrifying fang
It got such a scare
It sang a song that nobody could bear
Then for his behaviour, the ladybird got a dare
It was to visit a fire bear
Slowly, it came into the fire bear's lair
While he was eating his pears
The fire bear took his food, not willing to share
Then the ladybird got beaten,
Finally, the ladybird got eaten.

Abdullah Hussain (10)

Ivingswood Academy, Greenway

The Werewolf

It lies in Tilted Towers,
It takes a lot of showers
Absorbing power from the moon
Eating meat with a spoon
Jumping up high with a tie,
In the morning, he is a regular guy
That is shy
But at night, he has a hairy thigh
His name is Dire
Don't trust him because he's a liar
This werewolf always wakes up at night,
And wishes he could take flight.

Lincoln Savage (11)
Ivingswood Academy, Greenway

Singing Ladybird

A little ladybird singing loud,
Sitting high up on a cloud

It sings a tune,
Gets tired soon

It flies about,
Numerous shouts

It tried to come down,
But gets busy with sound

It's got a beautiful tone,
It always murmurs and groans

I soon find out it isn't singing,
The ladybird is shouting for help.

Zainab Zeeshan Butt (10)
Ivingswood Academy, Greenway

My Pet Genie

My pet genie can do everything,
Everything you want
Clap your hands twice,
And you'll see who will appear

Only three wishes a day,
And that's enough to say
That genie can do everything,
Any time of the day

In his lantern he goes,
Back to sleep
Ready for the morning,
In his bare feet.

Ayman Butt (10)
Ivingswood Academy, Greenway

Hear The Ladybirds Sing

The ladybirds
Singing so loud on the fluffy clouds
Humming and flying along the blue sky
Hopping and climbing on the tree,
Swaying and flapping their wings so high
All the ladybirds flying all day
But now it's time to lay all night
Tomorrow, the ladybirds will fly again.

Isha Mirza (10)

Ivingswood Academy, Greenway

Surfing On Lava

Surfing on burning lava,
Turning like the speed of sound
How, you ask? Well, on a magic board
That I leaned towards
Flying over the rocks
Reaching the biggest treetops
Then people saw me and called the cops
While cleaners were using mops
Then I flew down like a clown.

Izaac McConnell (10)
Ivingswood Academy, Greenway

I Licked A Pufferfish

I licked a pufferfish
My tongue swelled up
I felt sick
I thought I was going to die
My heart started to pound
I swam up in pain
I was rushed into hospital
I was fine so I was happy after,
Then I never swam in the sea again!

Mason Dickinson (11)
Ivingswood Academy, Greenway

Sunbathing On A Cloud

Once I was on a cloud,
It was very loud
I was so hot
It was like I was a wet mop
I ate a cloud made of mice
It was so nice
It was so hot
But I ate a lot
I cleaned my seat with a mop,
Then I saw a cop.

Zaina Riasat (10)
Ivingswood Academy, Greenway

Riding A Volcano

I went up to the volcano
Then the floor started shaking
So I jumped into it
And the lava pushed me up
I surfed down the rocky, bumpy hill
Called Bill
Until I slipped off my board!

Logan Jordan (10)
Ivingswood Academy, Greenway

Candyland

In Candyland, everything was made of sweets
Everyone was edible, you could eat your house
All the gingerbread people had lots of treats
There were lots of white chocolate mice
The mice scurried across the floor
And the chocolate birds soared

The roads were made of liquorice
And paths were made of biscuits
The trees were made of chocolate and green jelly
beans
A gingerbread had looked up and seen
A beautiful rainbow covered in sugar
It was surrounded with candyfloss clouds

There were statues of jelly babies,
And a lovely meadow of grated jelly beans
Everyone always smiled,
Because they smiled happily
People always said,
"Smiling makes a brighter day."

Nicole Hargreaves (10)
Long Meadow School, Milton Keynes

172

Foody Land

I live in Foody Land,
Where everything is good
I first went to Fast Food Frenzy
I ate the burger moon
Next, I went to Cookies 'N' Cream,
The best place to be
I went on a banana split,
Down a milk waterfall
I felt a twinge of guilt
For the people not here,
I went to bed on a marshmallow pillow
Then rhubarb came from very evil vegetables
Like a mustard seed, they grew
Then broccoli came to my rescue
They were good,
They ate up rhubarb in one gulp
"Hooray! We're saved!" said the people,
They were camouflages for the whole time,
I will give up eating and eat limes,
Because broccoli saved my life.

Joshua George (9)
Long Meadow School, Milton Keynes

The Genie

I jumped into a treasure box
Then I found a genie
But he was a meanie
He called me a fool
When I asked him for a swimming pool
I thought he was very cool

He was very loud
When I looked for him
He disappeared into the crowd
His house was small
But he was very tall
I asked him for a chocolate bar,
Instead he gave me a small car!
Which made me feel proud

The last thing I could wish for was
To get out and go home
So I said to him,
"I want to leave!"
But he said I could not
So I ran out the door

Then I was back at home
That was a fun time!

Anushree Pathak (10)
Long Meadow School, Milton Keynes

Water Wonderland

In Water Wonderland, there are bunnies,
Which are blue and pink
And that makes them think

There are chocolate rivers,
Which shimmer
Like glitter
Which means there's lots of litter

The pavement is made out of liquorice,
And the roads are made of biscuits
The trees are made out of chocolate and green
jelly babies

The clouds are made out of candyfloss
When you go up high or down low,
Who knows what you can eat?
And when it rains, who knows what you might eat!

Well, what is going to happen next?

Dhanvi Joy Choksi (10)
Long Meadow School, Milton Keynes

Num Num Land

There was an alien called Num Num,
She loved to do sums
She carried her sum book everywhere
And all the sumflies said,
"You're obsessed with maths!"

She was fantastic at cooking,
She loveed to do some looking
For some mathcorns
Mathcorns!

One day, Princess Mathcorn
Came to Num Num and said,
"Num Num, Num Num, what do we have here?
Would you like to be princess of Num Num Land?"

And to this day,
People tell the tale
Of how Num Num,
Became princess of Num Num Land!

Nana Nuru (9)
Long Meadow School, Milton Keynes

My Flying Bread Experience

I was putting on my jumpsuit,
And then my helmet too
I was going on my flying chocolate bread
And I was gonna zoom!

I flew over rock candy mountains,
And then over lollipop trees
In my hair there were candyfloss threads,
From me riding in the breeze

Then I took my seatbelt off,
Then I started surfing
Then I went through a cloud
That was weirdly burping!

I was leaving the realm of Wackyland
That I was going to miss
Since now I think that it was great,
I flew away to find another bliss.

Anna Batchelor (10)
Long Meadow School, Milton Keynes

Mermacorn Dance Party

I saw a mermacorn and it dragged me into the sea
As I screamed and yelled, "Wahee!"
It took me to her house in Candyland
Her house was made of cupcakes
And put together with chocolate spread
Then we stepped in her house,
Then ate a giant chocolate mouse
We stepped in the disco room
Then heard a great big *crash! Bang! Boom!*
Lala the mermacorn fell down,
She landed on her very own crown
We danced all night,
Then she wanted to fight
So I ran!

Jaysha Malika Coulthurst-Wood (9)
Long Meadow School, Milton Keynes

Billy's Water Party

W onderful letter came through the door
A n invitation to Billy's water party
T hen I got dressed and told my
E el that the party was at the big hole
R ummaging to get clothes for Eel

P lanet Cookie took me to the big hole
A fter we got there, we met Grape and Billy
R unning on the stage was Billy
T hen he said, "Let's dance, everybody!"
Y ears went by and he remembered it forever.

Evie Durn (9)
Long Meadow School, Milton Keynes

Marshmallow Bed

One day, I stepped into a room,
I'm so glad it didn't teleport me to the moon
Inside, I found a bed
"Cool," I said
I clambered inside,
I lay down
I definitely could not frown!
The duvet was as light as a feather,
I had never felt something as comfy, no never
I could smell the sweet, sugary, sticky air filling
each lung,
While I licked the mattress with my tongue
But now I couldn't hear a peep,
I was going to drift off to sleep.

Max Medley (10)
Long Meadow School, Milton Keynes

Chocolate Pool

I walked to school,
And I found the teacher was cool
She built an extension of a chocolate pool
Which was cool
The rule was cruel
But my friends thought it was cool
The head said I was cool,
So I thought he was a fool
The teacher said I was a meanie,
But I thought he was a genie
He was wearing a beanie,
He said I was loud
But it was a crowd
I felt proud
Just like a cloud
The clouds were cold
But they had mould.

Lily May Walsh (9)
Long Meadow School, Milton Keynes

Rainbow World

R iding a rainbow across the street
A mazed as I gazed
I suddenly saw a party ahead
N ever had I been to a party
B ut as I got there, they called my name
"O ver here, come on!"
W hen I got there, I was amazed

W hirled as I twirled
O bvious dancing with glee
R iding a rainbow in never-ending glee
L eading the way
D ancing the night away.

Imogene Rainbow Salamon (10)
Long Meadow School, Milton Keynes

Rainbow Cupcake

R unning on cupcakes
A ccidentally tripping
I had a wonderful time
N apping and
B asking on the cupcake
O ver the
W orld in delight

C arefully treading
U nder the sun
P eacefully sleeping
C arelessly jumping
A ll over the place
K arting around when suddenly
E ating the cupcake came into my mind and then
I ate it all!

Mohith Ram Sigirisetti (10)
Long Meadow School, Milton Keynes

Candyfloss Clouds

Once I had a trip to Candyfloss Clouds
I saw many people in big crowds
I got to swim with mermaids
In one of their big parades
Then I saw a chocolate dragon
Bigger than you could ever imagine!
I shape-shifted to a dragon
And when I flew, I saw a wagon
Filled with tourists and candy pets
Who were being taken to the vets
Later that day, I had to go back
I went away to my little shack.

Mia Farebrother (10)
Long Meadow School, Milton Keynes

Mané Mission

I decided to rob a bank
With Louis Vuitton unicorns
We took glittering jewels
And golden watches
And a limited edition Gucci bag
After we robbed the bank,
We met Salah with his humongous afro
He told us to help him find Mané
So we helped him and his crazy afro
We looked everywhere to find him
Until we found him in a cave playing Fortnite
Then it started to rain Gucci.

Logan George Freeman (9)
Long Meadow School, Milton Keynes

The Awesome Cat From Underground

In a forest that can't be found
There was a party underground.
I looked for something cool
But all I found was a school.
When I looked inside
I saw something that brought horror
It was a pixelated cat with circle feet!
So I went to investigate,
But soon I found he was a friendly cat
So we became best friends
And let our imagination run wild.

Dylan Jake Jemmett (9)
Long Meadow School, Milton Keynes

Beefy Brawl

I woke up standing,
When something was landing,
It was a sausage rainbow

Then came an army,
Who were all barmy,
They told me I had to go

They all were burgers,
Who committed some murders,
Their leader was called Mo

My rainbow was tasty,
But I had to be hasty,
Because I really needed to go.

Oheneba Kofi-Baah Dompreh (9)
Long Meadow School, Milton Keynes

188

Riding On A Lightning Bolt

As yellow as treasure and glittering stars,
The lightning bolt flashed as fast as a car
Shooting past the golden stars straight to Mars
While cars raced around the stars
The lightning bolt looked like a shining star in the
sky
It raced across the sky like a meteor shower,
The lightning bolt had an enormous amount of
power.

Alfie James Ratcliffe (9)

Long Meadow School, Milton Keynes

Pikachu

Pikachu is electric,
He can only say, "Pikachu!"
He is really small and cute
Not when you see him angry
He likes playing Minecraft
His favourite thing is bottle flipping,
He likes scaring people, shouting, "Pikachu!"

William Robertson (9)
Long Meadow School, Milton Keynes

YoungWriters®
Est. 1991

YOUNG WRITERS INFORMATION

We hope you have enjoyed reading this book – and that you will continue to in the coming years.

If you're a young writer who enjoys reading and creative writing, or the parent of an enthusiastic poet or story writer, do visit our website **www.youngwriters.co.uk**. Here you will find free competitions, workshops and games, as well as recommended reads, a poetry glossary and our blog. There's lots to keep budding writers motivated to write!

If you would like to order further copies of this book, or any of our other titles, then please give us a call or visit **www.youngwriters.co.uk**.

Young Writers
Remus House
Coltsfoot Drive
Peterborough
PE2 9BF
(01733) 890066
info@youngwriters.co.uk

Join in the conversation!
Tips, news, giveaways and much more!

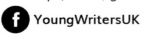 YoungWritersUK    @YoungWritersCW